First Facts™

Health Matters

Broken Bones

by Jason Glaser

Consultant:
James R. Hubbard, MD
Fellow in the American Academy of Pediatrics
Iowa Medical Society
West Des Moines, Iowa

Capstone
press®
Mankato, Minnesota

First Facts is published by Capstone Press
151 Good Counsel Drive, P.O. Box 669, Mankato, Minnesota 56002.
www.capstonepress.com

Library of Congress Cataloging-in-Publication Data
Glaser, Jason.
 Broken bones / by Jason Glaser.
 p. cm. — (First facts. Health matters)
 Includes bibliographical references and index.
 ISBN-13: 978-0-7368-6330-8 (hardcover)
 ISBN-10: 0-7368-6330-3 (hardcover)
 1. Bones—Wounds and injuries—Juvenile literature. 2. Fractures—Juvenile literature.
I. Title. II. Series.
RD101.G553 2007
617.4'71044—dc22   2006002808

Summary: Describes broken bones, how and why they occur, and how to treat and prevent
 them.

Editorial Credits:
Shari Joffe, editor; Biner Design, designer; Juliette Peters, set designer; Jo Miller, photo researcher;
 Scott Thoms, photo editor

Photo Credits
Capstone Press/Karon Dubke, 21
Corbis/Andrew Brookes, 14
Getty Images Inc./Photodisc Green/Russell Illig, 10–11; Sean Justice, 8; Stone/Charles Thatcher,
 15; Stone/Howard Kingsnorth, 6
Index Stock Imagery/Allen Russell, 9
PhotoEdit Inc./David Young-Wolff, 5
Photo Researchers, Inc./Gary Parker, 6 (inset); Salisbury District Hospital, cover (background);
 Science Photo Library/Mike Devlin, 17
Shutterstock/Chris Harvey, 20

1 2 3 4 5 6 11 10 09 08 07 06

Table of Contents

Signs of a Broken Bone

You heard a snap when you fell to the ground. Now your leg hurts so much that you think you might faint. The pain gets worse when you touch it. Something is pushing up against the inside of your skin. You have the signs of a broken bone.

Fact!

Kids fall a lot. They usually put their hands out to stop themselves. That's why kids break arms and wrists more than other bones.

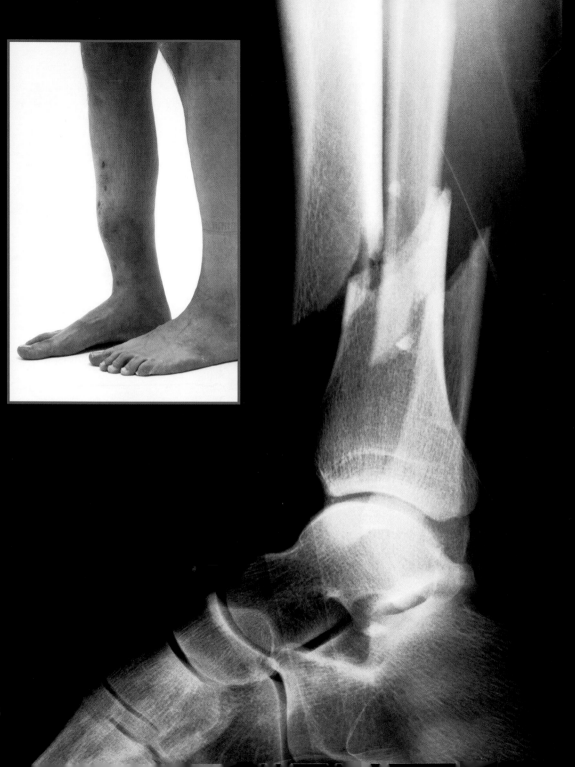

What Is a Broken Bone?

Our bones are very strong. They can handle a lot of weight and **pressure**. But too much pressure will cause a bone to break, or **fracture**.

A broken bone may have just a crack in it. Or it may snap all the way through, like a broken pencil. A bone can even get crushed into small pieces.

Fact!

When a broken bone sticks through the skin, it's called an open fracture. If it doesn't break through the skin, it's called a closed fracture.

How Do Kids Get Them?

A bone breaks when too much **force** is put on it. You might break a bone by falling onto hard ground or getting hit by a baseball.

Twisting or bending a bone too far can cause it to break. A bone can even break if too much weight lands on top of it.

What Else Could It Be?

Other injuries can look and feel like a broken bone. A **sprain** happens when muscles around a **joint** tear and swell.

Bones can **dislocate**, or pop out, where they come together at a joint. Dislocated bones can hurt as much as broken bones.

What to Do if You Break a Bone

You should see a doctor right away if you think you have a broken bone. Call an ambulance or have someone take you to the doctor. While you wait for help, hold the injured part still. If you have ice, use it to prevent swelling.

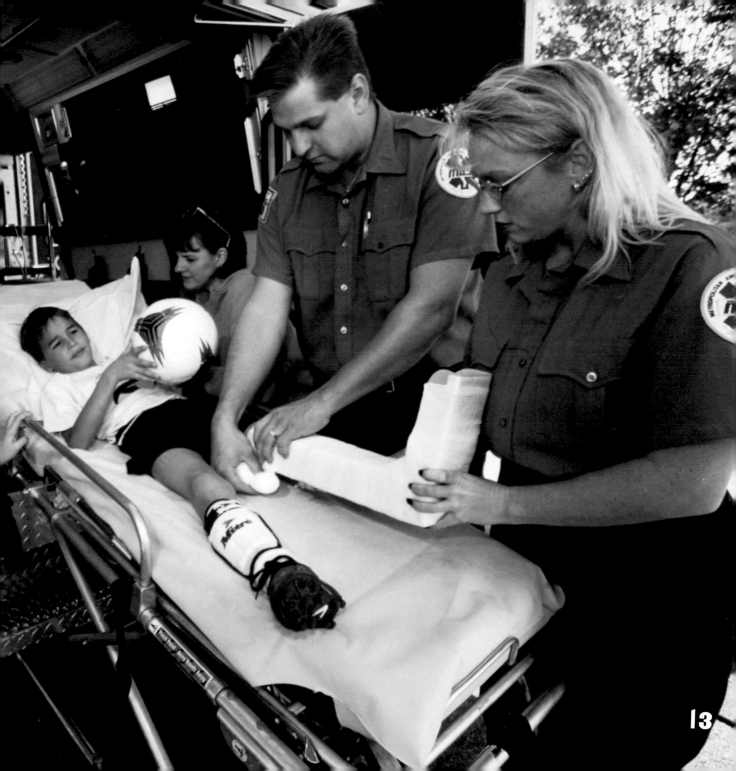

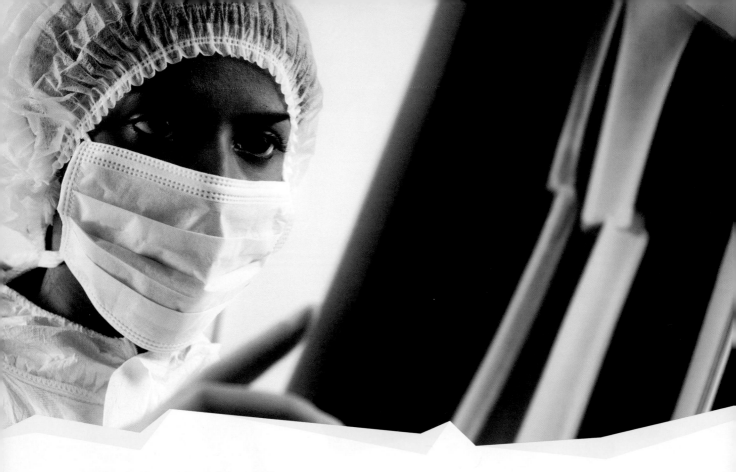

Treatment

Doctors take X-rays to see if bones are broken. Bones broken all the way through must be set. The doctor lines up the bone so it's straight again.

Casts are put on most broken bones. A cast keeps a bone from moving so it can heal. Over time, the bone grows back together.

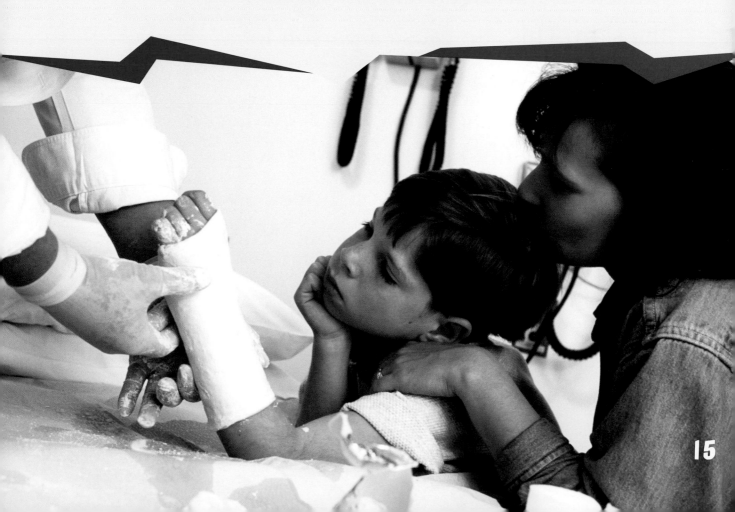

What Happens Without Treatment?

An unset broken bone may cut muscle. It may even tear through the skin. This can cause a person to lose blood.

A broken bone that is not treated quickly may not heal the right way. The bone may not grow or move correctly later on.

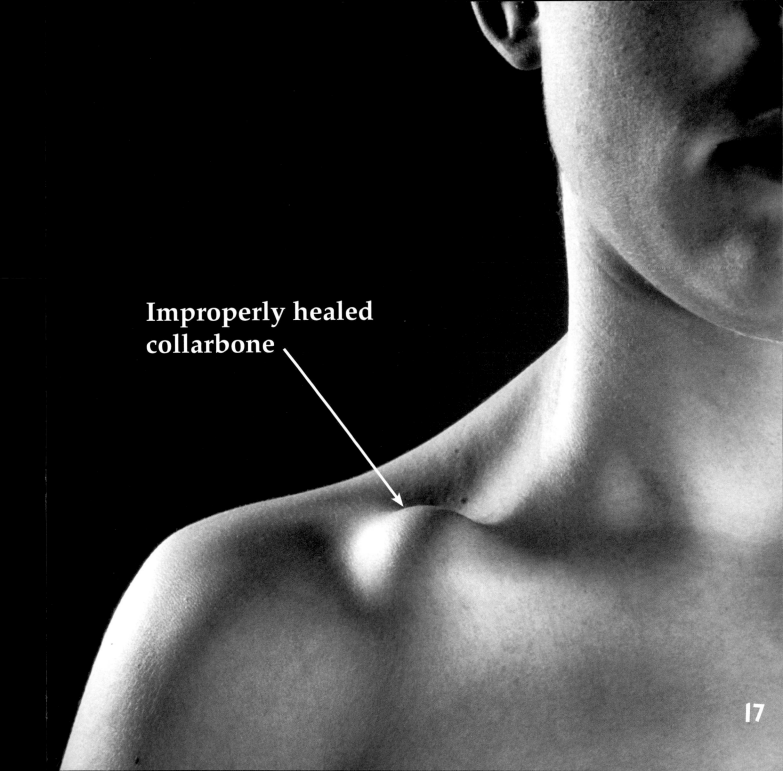

Improperly healed collarbone

17

Preventing Broken Bones

Exercise makes bones stronger. Yet many broken bones occur during sports. It is important to wear safety equipment while playing sports.

Always wear your safety belt in the car. Safety belts help protect you from getting broken bones during a car accident.

Fact!

Bones are made mostly from a mineral called calcium. Milk and other foods with calcium can make bones stronger and less likely to break.

Amazing but True!

The largest bone in your body could probably support the weight of a grand piano! Your femur goes from your hip to your knee. A healthy femur can support from 1,200 to 1,800 pounds (544 to 816 kilograms) without breaking.

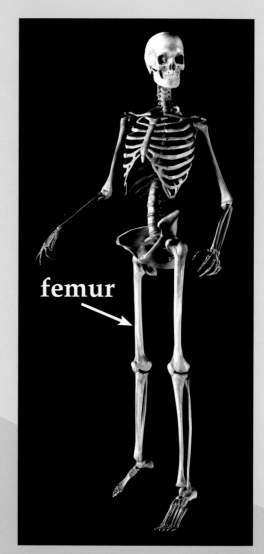

femur

Hands On:
Bone Structure

What You Need
2 paper-towel tubes
about 10 to 15 hardcover books
a friend

What You Do
1. Stand one cardboard tube up on a flat, level surface.
2. While one person keeps the tube steady, stack books on top of the tube until the tube collapses. Be careful when the books fall!
3. Take the set of books that were stacked on the first tube and remove one or two books. The idea is to have the most books the first tube held without collapsing.
4. While one person holds the tube steady, stack this set of books on top of the second tube.
5. Pinch the tube. Watch out! The books will quickly fall down as the tube bends.

   The cardboard tube is hollow. But it can hold the weight of many books. Many bones in our body are hollow, like the cardboard tube, but they are also strong. Your leg bones, for example, can support the weight of your entire body. But since your leg bone is hollow, it will break if hit hard enough from the side.

21

Glossary

cast (KAST)—a hard plaster covering that supports a broken bone

dislocate (DISS-loh-kate)—to separate a bone from the joint

force (FORSS)—strength or power; force is any action that changes the shape or movement of an object.

fracture (FRAK-chur)—a broken or cracked bone

joint (JOINT)—the place where two bones meet

pressure (PRESH-ur)—the force produced by pressing on something

sprain (SPRAYN)—an injury caused by muscle and tissue tearing near a joint

Read More

DeGezelle, Terri. *Your Bones.* Bridgestone Science Library. Mankato, Minn.: Bridgestone Books, 2002.

Gray, Susan H. *The Skeletal System.* Human Body. Chanhassen, Minn.: Child's World, 2004.

Royston, Angela. *Broken Bones.* It's Not Catching. Chicago: Heinemann Library, 2004.

Internet Sites

FactHound offers a safe, fun way to find Internet sites related to this book. All of the sites on FactHound have been researched by our staff.

Here's how:

1. Visit *www.facthound.com*

2. Choose your grade level.

3. Type in this book ID **0736863303** for age-appropriate sites. You may also browse subjects by clicking on letters, or by clicking on pictures and words.

4. Click on the **Fetch It** button.

FactHound will fetch the best sites for you!

Index